MW00904029

MAGNETIC TRUST

How Great Leaders Keep Top Performers and Get Extraordinary Results

By Dr. Heather Williamson

Dedication

This book is dedicated to the leader who is determined to be the best 'Damn Boss' he or she can be.

Acknowledgements

First, without the significant contributions made by each executive, this book probably would have taken a different route. I was truly blessed to have a group of executives share their experiences when building trust within their organizations.

Contributors to the book, Magnetic Trust: How Great Leaders Keep Top Performers and Get Extraordinary Results are:

John Ainsworth

David A. Christian

Nancy DeLisi

Mark Goad

Mary Jane Hogue

Dr. Nicolle Parsons- Pollard

Chris Shockley

Foster Taliaferro

Second, I would like to thank my awesome husband, Kent and son, Temple for being my biggest cheerleaders.

Magnetic Trust

How Great Leaders Keep Top Performers and Get Extraordinary Results

By Dr. Heather Williamson
#1 Bestselling Author

FREE – Check List

This book includes a **step-by-step checklist** to build Magnetic Trust in your leaders!

Table of Contents

Introduction
Welcome to Magnetic Trust!

This book represents nearly 20 years of education, hard work, experience and effort including client and executive stories. Maybe you're one of them, and if you are, thank you for your contribution!

Here is what to expect in this book so you get the most out of it and your expectations are met:

First, it's interactive. There are lots of opportunities for you to go deeper into the content and apply the concepts and strategies to help you develop trust skills and build trust among your team.

Second, this book is for business. It's intended to help you, as the boss, improve productivity, keep your top performers, grow your business, and of course, make money.

Third, it's for implementers. You'll see there are LOTS of ideas that you can use to improve employee productivity. However, I believe that becoming a leader, where developing trust within the team is the #1 priority, is where you need to start. Without employee trust, you are NEVER going to achieve the results you desire.

Fourth, this book wasn't intended to be a NY Times #1 Bestseller (although it is a #1 Best Seller). This is a book that's short for a reason, (so you read it), but it's packed with implementable content and lots of ideas. My intention, and the purpose of this book, is to show you the benefits of having employees that trust you as their leader, implement the trust building strategies into your business, and set yourself up for long-term growth. We have how-to strategies available that include everything you need to execute what you read in these pages.

Why Is Magnetic Trust Important?

"...No organization can take place without interpersonal trust, and no organizational leader can ignore the powerful element of trust."

~ Gilbert Fairholm

What is Magnetic Trust and how will it change the way you lead your employees?

I think the best way I can explain this is to paint you a picture...

Several years ago, I was working as a graduate assistant advising students on their academic majors while I was working on my Ph.D. I really enjoyed the job as I felt I was helping students plan their class schedules so they would graduate with their respective degrees.

In other words, I was helping them achieve their goals! (which, by the way, I love to do).

During my time as an academic advisor, I had the BEST boss! Dr. B always had a smile on his face and an open door. It didn't matter what the challenge was, he would provide support and guidance when needed.

I remember when one of our full-time colleagues, who we directly reported to, consistently tried to push her student advising workload on the graduate students. The workload became too much since we only worked twenty-hours a week. When the other graduate students approached Dr. B to share our concerns, he immediately took action letting the staff member know that she was full-time and as a result, should bear more of the student workload.

Now Dr. B could have taken the approach of' 'ya"ll work it out' but he recognized as a leader, it's important to do what's right. For Dr. B, that meant not playing favorites and holding staff accountable. Even though we were part-time employees, we were always treated equally and with respect. Consequently, as an employee, I always felt that he did the 'right' thing' for his employees, students, and university and thus, had employee trust.

In contrast, I want to share a couple more stories that demonstrate why developing trust is so important to your bottom-line, and also have an impact on retaining top talent.

It's also my reason for writing this book.

Many years ago, a sales manager was trying to motivate one of her employees to increase product sales in his territory. During this time, another one of her top sales representatives took a creative approach, and in an effort to increase store sales in her territory, was selling a joint promotion with a sister company. At the quarterly sales meeting, the sales manager recognized the low performing sales representative as the one who led the creative joint promotion and not the sales representative that actually implemented the offer.

OOPS, bad decision.

If you still don't understand how employee distrust occurs, here's another example:

It was summertime and one of the busiest times of the year at the local university. Summertime is busy because newly accepted freshmen are arriving to schedule their classes for the upcoming fall semester. The manager that oversaw all of the student advising within the College of Humanities had requested two weeks off to prepare for her daughter's wedding that was happening in several weeks.

Now there is an understood rule that no time off is allowed during new student orientation. However, she was granted approval to take the time off.

Now it just so happened that another employee was requesting two days off to move into a house that was just purchased. Interestingly enough, the spouse of the boss was also the realtor for the employee. However, this employee was denied leave and given the reason of the 'understood rule.'

In both scenarios, trust between the employee and the boss was broken. Employee trust was broken as a result of the boss being dishonest, showing favoritism, not treating everyone equally, downplaying the talents of others and refusing to apologize for mistakes or inappropriate behavior in an effort to protect his reputation.

Guess what was going through that employee's head?

Yep, you guessed it!

She was looking for what I refer to as "other opportunities" because she could no longer trust that her boss was looking out for her and NOT himself.

I know this to be true because, in both scenarios, that employee was ME. In the end, employees become emotionally attached to their boss. The degree of attachment varies based upon the level of caring, support, perceived value of contributions and internal job satisfaction.

I can share many more similar stories, but I think you get my point. In fact, you probably have your own horror boss stories as well, and if you don't, you are so very lucky.

In full disclosure, I have to let you know that these 'bad boss' stories are my WHY for doing what I do! There are so many high performing and motivated employees out there that truly want to be contributors to your business success.

I know this because I was one of them!

It's because of my experiences that I believe so strongly in coaching leaders on how they can create that 'Magnetic Trust' so that their top performing employees don't want to look for 'other opportunities.' Having had a boss that doesn't value and appreciate the skills and gifts that each employee has is my motivation to coach and educate.

So, I went back to school to get my education.

At the time I was newly married, (at thirty-two years old,) and quit a great paying job to finish my undergraduate degree, master's degree, and finally my Ph.D. For each of my degrees, I focused my research on leadership. Specifically, what makes a great leader and the negative impact of when a leader's behavior takes a detour into a less effective route.

This book is my way of sharing my knowledge and expertise in helping make YOU a GREAT LEADER. The first step to becoming that awesome leader is creating Magnetic Trust within your team and organization.

So, if this is one of the skills that you want to develop within yourself and implement back at the office, than you are in the right spot! I am here to show you the exact steps you can implement so you become that rockin boss and leader that I know you can become.

Still Not Sure? Check Out The Research

If you're like me, you probably hate reading research articles.

Yes, I'm a psychologist, and YES, I hate reading research articles.

So, I promise not to make this too painful. Personally, I like things simple, and I'm guessing you do as well.

The problem is this… Each day thousands of employees decide to voluntarily quit their jobs. Sometimes that is not a bad thing such as when the employee isn't a good fit or is under-performing.

In fact, I am sure you are doing the 'happy dance' as that employee is putting a drain on the team and your wallet.

It becomes a serious problem when you are seeing your top performing employees walk out the door. Believe me, these employees know they can find a better job with a much better boss.

So, they leave with a smile on their faces and also doing the 'happy dance.'

Just to put this in perspective for you, out of the **ten top motivators for employees** to stay in their job, **respect for their supervisor is consistently at the top of the list.** If you're like me, before I can respect my boss I have to trust him or her.

So, when your best employee walks out the door...

I am pretty confident that the next thought that comes to your mind is uh oh, I'm screwed!!!

Why? Because you're thinking, "my best employee(s) whom I trust, that gives 110% effort, holds himself accountable, makes good decisions, takes on tasks without being asked and does the job I pay him to do has now left me high and dry."

The next big question you should be asking yourself is not "who is going to do their job now," BUT rather "why did they leave?"

For one moment, I want you to forget about the expense you have now incurred as a result of your best employee saying goodbye. Even though the cost of an exit interview, advertising for job vacancy, training, loss of production and client revenues resulting from fewer clients being served because they haven't mastered the job yet[1], is significantly adding up.

What is really important to understand is that more than half of all managers do not trust their supervisor. Robert Hurley found this when he surveyed 450 executives from 30 companies around the world.[2]

Staggering I know!!!

A similar survey on ethics and workplace conducted by Deloitte in 2010 found that one-third of the participants would be looking for new jobs when the economy improved. Half of those employees stated that they distrusted their company.[3]

Well, guess what? The economy has improved.

I know you're thinking WHAT?!?! My best employee(s) is jumping ship the first chance that comes around???

---

[1]Of course I have to include my dissertation in this book 'The Link Between Transformational Leadership and Intent To Leave: The Mediating Role Of Trust" as it is the reason why I'm an Executive Coach.

[2]Check out Robert Hurley's article, 'Decision to Trust' in the Harvard Business Review September 20016 issue.

[3]Check out Catherine Capozzi's article, 'What Will Happen If Employees Do Not Trust Managers' in Chron.

Let me ask you this:

Would you be interested in learning the behavioral cues that suggest an employee doesn't trust you?

I thought you might say YES, so here are just a few:

- Lack of employee productivity
- Increased employee turnover
- Increased skepticism of manager
- Increased 'grape-vine' based communication
- Not being forthcoming to disclose problems and issues
- Showing up late to work
- Missed deadlines

So, now that you know the signs that your employee doesn't trust you…let's get to what this is REALLY costing you as a leader in your business. Trust is, and always will be, an economic influencer in your business.

It is time to accept what you may have been denying.

In their article, **The Connection Between Employee Trust and Financial Performance,** Stephen Covey and Douglas Conant write that the Great Place to Work Institute partners with *Fortune* to produce the "100 Best Companies to Work For" in which trust comprises two-thirds of the criteria. Their research shows that "trust between managers and employees is the primary defining characteristic of the very best workplaces." What's even more amazing is that these companies beat "the average annualized returns of the S&P 500 by a factor of three."

Still not convinced?

An advocacy group, **Trust Across America**, tracks the performance of America's most trustworthy public companies and has found that the most trustworthy companies have outperformed the S&P 500.

Last but not least, a 2015 study by **Interaction Associates** shows that high-trust companies "are more than 2½ times more likely to be high performing revenue organizations" than low-trust companies.[4]

Do you want to know why?

Here's your answer- Gallup found that companies with talented managers generally succeed at holding employee turnover to 10% or less annually, have 147% higher earnings and an 18% higher customer retention rate. All of which shows just how important employee retention is for your overall business success.

---

[4]Check out the article by Stephen Covey and Douglas Conant in the Harvard Business Review.

So, I hope by now you see the value and need for establishing Magnetic Trust between your managers and employees. As you can see, there are significant financial benefits to having a company culture that values and exhibits TRUST which results in keeping top performers.

Who am I and why should you listen to or trust me?

The **first reason** is because I know, from personal experience, the signs when an employee is THINKING about leaving the organization. How do you personally know, you ask?

I am that person.

My boss played favorites, awarded above the minimum salary increases to everyone on the team but me, lied about my performance to upper management, was vindictive, had a personal agenda, not receptive to any feedback from me, I could go on and on….

In the end, I felt demeaned, degraded, not valued, unappreciated and I even started questioning my own abilities (I got over that one quickly). Eventually, I had enough, so I 'checked out' and began counting down the days until I left.

The **second reason** is because I hold a Ph.D. in social psychology where I focused specifically on leadership.

Also, I have conducted multiple studies that examined these very management issues that have a huge impact on the business bottom-line. Areas such as what motivates employees, the impact of employee distrust, how values influence performance and WHY employees leave what is perceived to be a great company. (Spoiler alert- it's the boss.)

The **third reason** is because I have been coaching executives, business owners, and managers for over ten years. During this time, I have seen it all. From the micro-manager who doesn't trust his team to make an informed decision to managers that use intimidation and manipulation as a strategy to increase performance, (and then wonder why it's not working…)

Bottom-line, I know what I'm talking about.

The **fourth reason** is that a recent article in the Wall Street Journal reported that due to the strong economy and record low unemployment, 3.4 million people voluntarily quit their jobs in April 2018, according to the Labor Department figures.

That, my friend, is a LOT of people!

So, if you are open to receiving insight and strategies from someone who knows a thing or two about building Magnetic Trust and a high performing team, then I am your girl!

If not, then I wish you much success in figuring out why your top performing employees are leaving your company. If you need help down the road, I am here for you.

So, are you ready to start building Magnetic Trust with your employees?

Alright then. Let's get started!

The Role Of Trust

Our **lives are built on trust relationships**. We trust payroll to deposit our paychecks into our checking accounts, (it would be devastating if we were writing checks and there wasn't any money in the account). We trust that delegated tasks are completed by colleagues and staff. Finally, we trust that the motives behind our supervisors' behavior are honest and not self-serving or vindictive. [5]

I mean, is it really too much to ask to have your supervisor support and value you as an employee?

I think NOT.

So, you're probably asking yourself, 'What is Magnetic Trust that this Dr. Heather keeps referring to?'

Well, let me tell you.

Magnetic Trust occurs when there is an unexplainable force that pulls you toward your boss.

---

[5]Yes, I'm pulling from my dissertation again.

Have you ever thought to yourself… I trust 'Ted' but I can't explain why. I just know that whatever he asks me to do, I will do it and give 110% (legally of course.)

This pulling force is real. You are pulled toward the will of your boss because you KNOW that he/she has your best interest at stake, puts you in roles that allow you opportunities to grow both personally, and professionally, and because your boss is your Supporter-in-Chief, (your personal cheerleader,) a level of comfort is experienced.

When Magnetic Trust exists, there is authenticity, trustworthiness and reliability. These attributes become an expectation of your employee and a personal obligation for you, the boss, to exhibit.

In fact, when Magnetic Trust in the leader exists, the quality of communication and problem-solving improves, the discretionary effort of the employees increases, along with their job commitment. Last, but not least, the voluntary employee turnover decreases[6], which means your employees aren't leaving you high and dry. YAY!!!!

In a nutshell, Magnetic Trust forms the foundation for effective communication, employee retention, em-

---

[6]Yes and yes I'm again pulling from my dissertation

ployee motivation and the extra effort (that 110%) that is expended on tasks. This is because your employees have faith in your directives, instructions, values and company vision.

Without Magnetic Trust between you and your staff, it will be extremely difficult to have your ideas accepted. That literally would 'bite the big one!'

One thing that you truly need to understand is that Magnetic Trust doesn't just happen. You can't wave a magic wand and poof! Your employees aren't suddenly going to trust everything you say and do. Trust is something that is earned over time through consistent practice of trusting behaviors or the **Magnetic Rules**.

To help you in earning Magnetic Trust of your employees, I want to share some rules that you can implement today and every day that will get you the employee results you want, expect and deserve.

MAGNETIC
TRUST RULES

ere are the Magnetic Trust Rules that you, as a leader, should be exhibiting with your team, on a daily basis. I can promise you that if you choose not to exhibit one or more of them, lack of trust will be the result. **It's all or nothing**.

Magnetic Trust Rule #1: Be Authentic

Magnetic Trust Rule #2: Be Predictable

Magnetic Trust Rule #3: Be Transparent

Magnetic Trust Rule #4: Exhibit Ethics

Magnetic Trust Rule #5: Communicate, Communicate, Communicate

Magnetic Trust Rule #6: Own it, Don't Blame it

Magnetic Trust Rule #7: Show Competence

Magnetic Trust Rule #8: Don't Play Favorites

THESE MAGNETIC TRUST RULES WILL WORK FOR YOU AND WITH YOUR TEAM!

However, these rules work ONLY *when you implement all of them*!

Think about it this way: I bet in the beginning, each one of your employees once hired, showed up to work excited to try and make an impact, whether large or small, in your business. Each one of your employees acted this way because they wanted to feel they are contributing in some way towards your success.

When one or more of your employees STOPPED feeling this way, this was when the STRUGGLE and FRUSTRATION began for you.

In fact, I was having dinner with a friend of mine, who holds an executive level position in a fast growing company. He recently shared the growth challenges his company was experiencing in the pharmaceutical industry. The number one challenge for the executive team to move in the right direction was gaining employee trust and confidence. This challenge also impacted the level of work performance.

My friend understands that once trust is established, implementing the appropriate processes and strategies would be much easier. Plus, it allows the employees to work more efficiently across departments, which ultimately improves employee work performance.

Ken Blanchard, (one of my favorite leadership gurus,) recently looked at the relationship between trustworthy leadership behavior and productive employees and found that **45% of employees say, "lack of trust in leadership is the biggest issue in work performance."**

OUCH!!

I guarantee you that if you don't have employee trust, you're not going to have a high performing team!

In an effort to share the importance of developing Magnetic Trust with your employees, I thought you would get some value if I shared the perspectives of other executives and business owners, just like yourself from diverse industries. So, I will be highlighting one company for each 'Magnetic Trust Rule' and share WHY they think a specific Rule is important and how they implement Magnetic Trust building strategies within their company.

So, let's get started.

Magnetic Trust Rule #1: Be Authentic

have this as Rule 1 for a reason. Personally, I believe that being 'Authentic' in your efforts to build trust is a requirement. When you are 'FAKE' in showing you care about your employees' feelings or pretend to be engaged in their daily activities, people see right through it. Without authenticity, all your efforts to create trust with your staff will be in vain.

As a leader, when your interactions with your employees are purported to be authentic but in reality, are self-serving, your team sees right through you.

I'm going to say it again…as a leader, when your interactions with your employees are purported to be authentic, but in reality are 'self-serving', your employees see right through you.

So, stop being a JERK! (of course, I say this with love).

Always remember that your ACTIONS speak louder than your WORDS.

Dr. Nicolle Parsons-Pollard, Vice Provost for Academic and Faculty Affairs at Monmouth University, shared her perspective on the importance of being **_authentic with employees_** and the impact it has when building Magnetic Trust within her university.

**Dr. Nicolle chose the Magnetic Trust Rule: Being Authentic when building employee trust** because she believes employee trust is needed in order to make anything else happen within the organization.

Being authentic includes how you operate daily, lead and make decisions. When you are authentic the employee may not agree with the decision you make but it lets them clearly know who you are.

Being 'authentic' also gives people the opportunity for them to be themselves as well or be their best personal self. The outcome of being 'authentic' is it allows others to be authentic as well.

Sometimes as a woman and a minority, you believe that you have to show up in a particular type of way in *order to get the same level of respect as a man. I have discovered that it is very hard not to be who you are for any length of time. This even applies to cocktail parties that your colleagues are attending. So, it's important to figure out a way to allow your best self to show up.*

At Monmouth University, the idea of my race and how it impacts others and how they respond to me has not been an issue, even though I am the only African-American who has held the Vice Provost position. I have been very fortunate and appreciate that I can be my authentic self.

Understanding what I believe and who I am and doing that every day in everything that I do.

Dr. Nicolle practices being **authentic by:**

- Making herself vulnerable. Dr. Nicolle believes that if you don't know an answer, say you don't know.

- Own your mistakes when made and apologize, (this isn't the norm,) but it allows people to see that you are human.

- Allow people not to be perfect by providing a safe environment to learn from mistakes as this promotes innovation and creativity.

- Let people know it's ok not to play it SAFE.

- Allow the team to share opinions and not just say it because you are the administrator or boss.

- Give credit for contributions and opinions when their suggestions are implemented. It's not about checking the box that a topic was discussed but **authentically** wanting to hear what others have to say.

- Emphasize when you don't have all of the answers, so, be open to welcoming feedback.

Dr. Nicolle believes that the #1 thing a leader should know about 'Being Authentic' when building employee trust is *when times are tough or controversial issues arise, don't worry about how your response makes you look. It's important to be open and share where you're coming from.*

As a leader it imperative that you be able to separate personal views from professional views. Also, don't be afraid to share personal stories as it helps people connect with you. Part of being a leader is being able to connect with individuals so that they will be interested in hearing about what your objective is.

It's about being influential.

If you're not influential as a leader, then you are not leading anyone at all. You're just taking a walk by yourself.

So, allow yourself to be vulnerable and not afraid to expose things that are personal in nature to make a connection with people. Most of my ability to connect with people comes when I have one-on-one meetings with people where we deviate from what the objective is. They may look different and I ask, "are you feeling ok?"

That's when people open up and share what is happening in their life. At this time, they realize that you care about them as a person and not just the work they do for you. Understand that we are complete individuals. Let your team know that, 'I get it, it happens to me too.' We're human. When you are able to be 'authentic' it returns back in dividends. Being 'authentic' allows for a better understanding of errors in judgment and in turn they will want you to be a better leader.

The return on being 'authentic' is invaluable!!!! People honestly want you to do well as a leader and in return it frees everyone up to be better.

The last piece of advice Dr. Nicolle would like to share is it's so important to use honesty as the underlying culture that allows people to share their thoughts.

If you can feel comfortable in telling your boss that he did something wrong....

It's the beginning of any relationship whether personal or professional. If you're unwilling to be authentic, the relationship will be built upon a foundation that is fragile. Also, people don't want to work as hard for someone they don't like very much. You are far more likely to be well received in how you make decisions which also makes your employees world more stable. No one likes instability.

Magnetic Trust Rule #2: Be Predictable

Think back to when you were an employee and had to approach YOUR boss about an issue. Did you know how he was going to respond? Were you hoping it was going to be a good day and he wasn't going to 'go off' because you knocked on his door?

Mark Goad, Associate Broker with Coach House Realty, shared his **perspective on how being predictable impacts building Magnetic Trust with his team.**

Mark stated that being predictable was, "one of the things that has been most challenging for me in my sales career as I am very much a free spirit. Having structure has been a challenge but now I see the value and it's importance and have worked hard at developing the skill."

According to Mark, you can become more **predictable** as a leader when you are:

- Set clear expectations, so that your employees clearly understand what you want from them.

- Be available at the same time, not necessarily all the time but at consistent times. Being predictable also provides a level of comfort even if someone knows that they can't get an answer to a question, or problem can't be solved that very minute, just knowing when they can get that help provides a level of comfort, versus wondering when, or if, you ever get to connect.

- Treat each person and situation consistently. When you do this, it doesn't take people very long to know what to expect from you. Especially, when a person comes to you with an issue or question when you're consistent about it. Mark believes this offers a 'layer of comfort' for the employee.

- Follow-up with a handwritten note afterwards whenever you meet or call a staff member.

- Be available. Be clear when you're not available and what to do if you're not there in those instances. Let your employees know that you are there for them when they need guidance. Also, when you are out of the office or in meetings, let your people know who to contact for solutions, or that you trust in their decisions.

- Hold regularly scheduled meetings and make sure you share the agenda ahead of time in both team and individual meetings. Be sure to share input of what is happening in the company and not have surprises. It's extremely important to not play games and hide things unnecessarily. Basically, don't pull big surprises on people. Your employees don't like it and it diminishes trust.

- Keep the same demeanor when someone comes with a situation by turning off what is in your head, and focus on them exclusively. Make them feel like they're the only one in the room. I want my people to know they have my undivided attention when they need me. This can be accomplished by turning away from computer and putting away the cell phone when you meet.

Mark feels that **being predictable with your employees** *is one of the most important characteristics when building Magnetic Trust and unfortunately the most overlooked. Mark understands that employees need to know what is expected of them when approaching their leader. Which personality they'll get or when you'll get back with the employee about an issue they* *need help with. If you are unpredictable, it drives people away. Not just when or if you are going to respond but how you will react.*

You know what I mean... Is today your psycho day?

So, as a boss being predictable means how you communicate AND how you behave.

Magnetic Trust Rule #3: Be Transparent

When I was working in sales for Philip Morris USA, we would get monthly directives on our promotional goals. My boss, Sonny, was great at sharing what the expectations were for our territories without 'sugar coating' or hyping up the sales numbers.

With Sonny, we knew that 'what you see is what you get.' There weren't any games played and if we shared that a specific promotion was not going to be well received, due to consumer demographics, he shared that with management. As a team, we gave **110%** effort because we trusted Sonny to be honest and transparent with us and knew that he had our backs, and we in turn, had his.

My personal level of trust for him is so strong, that we still stay in touch and I believe that he and his wife are my 'second parents.'

That, my friends, is a personal testimonial to the positive impact of transparency. Don't just take my word for it, here is another leader's perspective:

John Ainsworth, President & CEO with CULedger and Former Executive Vice-President of North America Markets with Mastercard, shared his perspective on the importance of *being transparent with employees,* and the impact it has when building Magnetic Trust.

John suggests that there are four areas to look at when measuring transparency and having dialogue with employees. The four areas are: Partnership, Trust, Agility and Initiative.

John believes that transparency goes back to expectations. We, as leaders, need to have a clear line of communication with the employee and be transparent in what we expect from them in their job role. When an employee is new to the role (less competent), more specific 'hand-holding' or support may be needed. This includes a lot of communication that involves being included in the decision process. Supporting decisions may include being the resource for a sales employee when he has to confront an executive regarding meeting missed product deadlines.

In comparison, when the employee has more experience, he may only need to be directed to find out what resources are needed or what objectives are trying to be achieved such as pricing structure or policy approval. This level of expectation involves regular check-ins to see if the employee is on track.

The last level is delegating. This occurs when the employee comes to leadership when a problem exists and they don't know how to resolve it or achieve it, and you as the leader help guide in the process.

As a leader it's important to understand what level of support the employee requires. Once the level of support is known, communicating the 'transparency' of expectations can be established, and are understood upfront. If you're not transparent, and not clear with expectations, the employee relationship doesn't end well.

According to John, leaders can be 'transparent' with their team by:

- Being transparent and clear in terms of unit goals (i.e., revenue, market share, sales, product).

- Being transparent on company challenges such as being #2 in the market.

- Being transparent on performance and how you are being measured. (It involves trust and partnership). It's important to be transparent on what your employees are doing well and also areas where there is an opportunity.

- Having the mindset and internal strength to exhibit a 'What you see is what you get' transparency.

According to John, *the #1 thing a leader should know about 'Being transparent' when building employee trust is NOT to confuse transparency with trust. It doesn't mean that if I am transparent with an employee and we have open communication that they trust me to deliver on what I've communicated or signed up for. It also doesn't mean that I have trust for them either.*

Those are two very different perceptions.

Just because you may be honest and transparent, that doesn't mean it equates to trust.

In my current role as president of a start-up, I believe that Trust is the most important thing we need to have because decisions happen fast. I need to have the client mindset be that I'm not going to let you fail, I will adapt and be agile so the client achieves success.

The last piece of advice John would like to share is there is a difference between trust and friendship. The people you have the most trust in at times may also be considered a friend. When this occurs, an unhealthy emotional turmoil in the workplace is experienced as a result of not wanting to upset the friendship. Because the friend is the go-to person in the work relationship transparency tends to go too far and the decisions made may not be what's best for the company.

Magnetic Trust Rule #4: Exhibit Ethics

Exhibiting ethical behavior is a VERY important rule when establishing trust as a supervisor.

When I was teaching a business leadership course at Virginia Commonwealth University, (Go Rams!), and the topic of ethics was covered, I would bring in current examples of national and local leaders convicted of embezzlement, fraud, harassment and other crimes, (we all know who Bernie Madoff is.) I shared these examples of when leaders chose personal gain over what was right and ethical and the consequences of their decisions. It served as a visual reminder of the impact those decisions made on their life and family. In fact, it made for great discussions on how leaders can act ethically when temptations exist, which of course was the purpose.

This leads me into the next topic of how you can exhibit ethical behaviors and become a role model to your team.

David A. Christian, Former Vice-President and Chief Innovation Officer with Dominion Energy, shared his perspective on the importance of **exhibiting ethics with employees** and the impact it has when building Magnetic Trust.

When attracting millennial talent to Dominion Energy, there are four reasons why you would want to work for us. The first is the mission. The mission is serving the public and our customers, twenty-four seven and 365 days of the year. We are part of both the Virginia and nation's economy, national security and it's super important.

The second reason is ethos. We communicate four values at every meeting which include: safety, ethics, excellence and teamwork. Our people are trained on these values and leadership is expected to reflect and model the value attributes.

When exhibiting ethics, for me, that not only means doing the right thing but also having the appearance of doing the right thing, which is fair dealing with everyone.

Doing the right thing means conformance of rules and standards and is our ethical floor for doing business. In comparison, the appearance of doing the right thing is just as important because if people misinterpret your actions, however well-meaning, it doesn't help to build that trust.

For us at Dominion Energy, we look at ethics two ways, Inside Ethics and Outside Ethics. Outside Ethics, (outside the company,) focuses on doing right by the environment and stewardship for the environment, in which we seek to exceed the minimum standard.

Another attribute is to provide our employees the opportunity to volunteer in the community (Outside Ethics). We have teams that seek to do good in the environment.

The third attribute focuses on inside the company, (Inside Ethics,) by providing the opportunity to allow employees to do important and meaningful work within the company.

The fourth attribute, (Inside Ethics,) is investment in employees and recognizing there is always a market for excellence. We invest in employees so they stay with us and to limit turnover.

When it comes to 'exhibiting ethics' with his team, David believes that:

Employees need to understand the WHY's of decisions being made and provided with the fuller perspective of the WHY and not what is just in the newspaper. Strategies that David implemented to exhibit ethics included:

- Having management meetings every two months and talking about the good, bad and ugly. These discussions included what we were doing really well, where we were falling short and needed to have some corrective action plans and finally things that were not meeting standards.

- Taking the opportunity to explain why certain decisions are being made and listening to the perspectives of employees and answering their questions, being available for, and taking the jabs when needed.

- Exhibiting ethical behavior. Remember there are thousands of eyeballs watching what you do and listening to what you say. When talking with leadership, I would ask them to think about the most influential people in their life, (mother, father, grandparent.) Ask the questions again but refer it to their work life. The answer is often not

the chairman, but rather their immediate supervisor or one level above. It's important to recognize how much influence they have on others.
As a leader, you're a teacher no matter what, and
always "ON." Your staff watches what you say,
and watches what you do, and then decides on
that basis how to act. Know that your influence
is greater than you perceive it to be.

- Talking with leadership and employees consistently. This allows you to better understand what
employees are thinking.

- Recognizing the importance that everyone brings
to the job, no matter what level. I would stop and
shake their hands and thank everyone for their
contributions. Simply showing appreciation for
the contribution that people are making at every
level builds management credibility, and ultimately people expend the discretionary effort
within the team toward the mission.

- Being a cheerleader for the team. Communicate
constant positive reinforcement, walk around
the office, plant yourself in one spot, then change
walking patterns, and bring others to share in the
'walk' and share their observations.

- Teaching people the right way to go so they
are successful. Incorporate continuous learn-

ing as part of our principles. Even make discipline productive by turning it into a teaching opportunity by making the behavior change clear.

- Being enthusiastic by doing cheers, reminding people that enthusiasm is contagious. If we could build enthusiasm around the work people are doing and build trust, it would translate into the discretionary effort needed. This can be accomplished by providing direction, building alignment, and commitment. As a method to achieve enthusiasm, we incorporate jumping jacks, push-ups, and other shared team experiences as activities to build our team.

According to David, the #1 thing a leader should know about 'exhibiting ethical behaviors' when building employee trust is:

First, know that people watch what you do and listen to what you say, and then they decide on that basis how to think and act. Think about the saying, 'What you do speaks so loudly that I can't hear what you say.' Make sure your behaviors match your words.

Second, people don't understand the degree of influence they have, and are constantly underestimating it. Keep in mind that as a leader you are constantly in a teaching mode, whether it's acknowledged, or not.

The last piece of advice that David would like to share is on the importance of building trust through ethics.

David believes that it is important to provide opportunities where staff and management can volunteer alongside one another, away from site, and to invest in your people. These actions will allow you to see returns many times over.

In sharing a final thought, David shares a story (which I personally love!!!)-

"A plant manager was going to share a few words at the retirement of one of his employees who was a machinist. The plant manager goes to HR and looks at the employee file and discovers that he's been with the company for thirty-five years. At the retirement he wishes him all the best and asks him sheepishly if he would like to share a few words. The plant manager is reluctant to hand over the microphone. Joe takes the microphone and says, 'for thirty-five years you have paid me for the work of these hands, but I gladly would have given you what's in my head and in my heart for the same wage if you had only asked."

Get the head and heart together from each employee and this is where you will get their discretionary effort.

Trust gets built by getting everyone on the team engaged so they feel part of a team. David says that he was known to be very tough, but fair. "My job is not to do anything that will lose respect. By focusing on having respect eliminates favoritism."

Magnetic Trust Rule #5: Communicate, Communicate, Communicate

'What we have here is a failure to communicate'

~Cool Hand Luke

I use this quote whenever I teach a workshop on communication because it is one of the number one challenges in companies today. Of course, the movie was awesome too! Who doesn't like Paul Newman?

Mary Jane Hogue, Chief Innovation Officer with MEDARVA, shared her perspective on the importance of consistent **communication with employees** and the impact it has when building Magnetic Trust.

Mary Jane chose the Magnetic Trust Rule: Communicate, Communicate, Communicate when building employee trust because she believes we are better when we communicate, especially when we communicate face to face. Mary Jane sees that the way the digital world impacts our time together may not be as positive as it could be. For example, we spend the first part of our day answering emails that we received overnight. Some of the emails may involve a complicated question from a colleague or staff member whose desk is around the corner from your desk. Rather than requesting a meeting, or walking in to talk about the issue, an email is sent.

Mary Jane believes that face time with staff is more productive and clarifying because it allows the ability to see the expression on someone's face, if they are confused, or if they have an 'ah ha' moment, or they think you are just absolutely wrong. Face-to-face communicating allows the opportunity to adjust in the give and take of a conversation.

We need to work more on stronger internal communications with one another as a way to share more effectively what we are doing as businesses with the outside world.

When it comes to *implementing consistent 'communication' with her team,* Mary Jane utilizes several strategies:

- When a question arises, model your expectation by getting out of your chair, and going to the employee for clarification, allowing a face-to-face conversation, rather than sending emails, which can cause more confusion.

- When holding weekly staff meetings, make it a point NEVER to do all of the talking. The focus is on the staff and they would share what they are working on, feelings of success, current challenges, and finally what they are feeling overwhelmed about. As a team, we would jump in and help the employee strategize for solutions.

- Team building exercises were held yearly where we learned one another's strengths and weaknesses. It was a tool to learn how my team perceived my communication skills as well as each other's. It was an opportunity to improve so that I was a better peer and leader.

- Schedule time out of the office for lunch to celebrate birthdays and project successes so that we could bond and better understand each other outside the office. This was a huge success, we became stronger inside the office as we communicated more.

- Encourage staff to know it's ok to have conversations when experiencing challenges, this helps to create a cohesive openness.

- Have entire non-profit staff attend   board meetings when possible as it's beneficial that we are all hearing the same message.

- Communicate board goals so everyone is on board to be a cohesive team.

- Customer service- put your best hat on to be attentive to the ask or concern for anyone that called or walked through the door.

Mary Jane believes that the #1 thing a leader should know about 'communicating' with staff is

to be honest and open. When communicating honestly show compassion, gratefulness and make sure that every employee understands their true value and importance within the organization. If you share that you care about your employee, it will be reciprocated in a positive way.

It is difficult to just share one piece of wisdom. So, I am not.

When considering communication, the second piece of advice I would share is that it's also important to do more listening than talking. By listening more than talking, we learn more about what our employees are thinking, feeling and their desires.

This is GOLD!

If I had a fault, it's expecting the same level of honesty from colleagues and staff when communicating with me. Employees shouldn't be reluctant to share when a mistake is made, but rather understand it's ok to make mistakes as they can be fixed.

Finally, it's important as a leader to be helpful. For instance, if you have two ends of the cooler no matter who is in the office or what your positions is, pick up the other end of the cooler to help the other colleague out. These non-verbal actions resonate with the team even though it wasn't spoken. Don't ever think just because you are the boss, that you are too good to help a team member out when needed.

The last piece of advice that Mary Jane would like to share is that in *today's tumultuous age, it's important to communicate the positive actions more frequently and with ease rather than the negative actions.*

For example, communicate the good things to your team member such as, "Jane, thank you so much for all that you did today. Because of what you do or initiated or completed, it meant so much to me and the organization." We don't do enough pats on the back and it's a shame. Not only will the compliments increase employee effort but they can also filter down at home too.

How fantastic would that be?

So, start communicating more frequently, and make sure that whatever you are saying, your actions (non-verbals) are in alignment. When your actions are not aligned, that is when mixed messages are sent and trust can deteriorate.

Magnetic Trust Rule #6: Own it, Don't Blame it

Picture this scenario in your mind…

As a sales executive, one of the biggest new product launches has been running for a month. The sales reports are in and you notice the revenue is not where it had been projected.

What do you do?

Do you blame the sales representatives for not working hard enough?

Or

Do you go back and look at the product to see if improvements can be made or if the customer even wants it?

Owning successes AND failures is important when you are leading a team. It's easy to take credit when things go your way such as the product kick-off sold 1000 units or customer feedback is saying how great you are. However, it's really tough when sales revenue isn't what was projected or a product launch was a dud.

So how do you respond?

Do you accept responsibility or do you pass the buck and blame an employee or department?

Foster Taliaferro, Senior Operations Executive with Reconserve Inc., shared his perspective on how **owning what you do and say and not blaming mistakes on others** impacts building Magnetic Trust with his team.

Foster strongly believes that Leadership starts at the top. (I, of course, happen to agree with him).

As a leader within his company, Foster understands that it's easy to blame others for problems but blaming others doesn't fix the problem. Even when previous management dropped the ball and blamed other people. Foster believes that as a boss, you must own the problem, whether it's poor communication, lack of team building, or silos within the company.

Foster believes it's his job to inspire the front-line managers by not focusing on what happened yesterday but instead, "what are we doing today." He believes in owning past leadership mistakes, and understands that if you don't own them, then you're shirking responsibility and not solving the problem.

Jokingly, Foster shared that when you're pointing a finger or blaming others for a problem, you have three fingers pointing back at you. So be careful when pointing a finger or placing blame.

It's important to develop a culture/environment for success. That can be accomplished by having an owning mentality rather than a blaming mentality. When we all 'own' our decisions it makes the company better.

Foster believes that you can begin to 'own' decisions by:

- Being very 'hands on' and present with your team. Show empathy in what is needed to get the job done but don't do their job.
- Walking around the 1st hour of the morning, and talking to your team, and help out when you see an employee struggling. As a leader, you should want to understand the team's job and you can't do that from an office.

- Leading by example. When they see me helping the team, I hope that next time an employee may exhibit the same behaviors, by helping others when needed.

- It's important to encourage the team to be brave and think outside the box to make their job easier while supporting their ideas when finding better ways to do things.   By allowing the team to present their 'ideas' it promotes the opportunity to prove or disprove. If the ideas are good ones, then supporting them by allocating resources. This allows the employee(s) to own the idea and implement it if accepted.

Go with it and run with it!

We promote the belief "let's not just get by but get better!" Don't be satisfied with the status-quo.

I feel that people are craving to be led and not managed.

It's my responsibility as their leader to lead the team by owning not only past management decisions whether they were good or bad.

Foster believes that the #1 thing a leader should know about 'owning and not blaming' others is *that the goal is to get everyone pointed in the same direction,*

being empathetic and not managing from a glass ceiling. This can be accomplished by treating everyone the same. That means showing respect to everyone, from the guy that sweeps the floor, to the CEO of the company. It's important, every day, to bring in the belief that everyone can be a leader. Ensure the team has the tools and time, be empathetic and be real.

Bottom line...it starts with the belief, 'Say what you mean and mean what you say.'

My goal is to develop leadership in everyone. If you lead people will follow, if you don't, they won't.

The final piece of advice that Foster would like to share is that your employees are craving to be led, not managed. Leaders employ people to do their job, while managers have to oversee everyone.

I view myself as a good leader and a fair manager. I would rather be that way.

It's simple... Lead and they will follow, set high standards and hold people accountable for their areas of responsibility. Have your people lead and make decisions (even when in doubt) and encourage them to own it. Don't penalize them if it's wrong but use it as an opportunity to learn.

It's all about the people at the end of the day!

Regardless of whether you're managing a call center, managing staff responsible for developing a product, or supporting a team that manages operations, it's all about the people.

It's a leader's job to get at the core of what makes your employees tick. How do you inspire people to achieve more than they thought they could.

Once you understand this, you manage less because you're now leading.

I view myself as a successful leader when I see my front-line managers leading their groups, getting them to break down the walls and silos between them and 'owning' the decisions made.

Magnetic Trust Rule #7: Show Competence

As a leader, don't you think your employees want to believe you understand and possess knowledge of your industry and business?

Well of course your employees want this and deserve it. That was a rhetorical question…

It can definitely be a challenge to get your employees on board, because they want to, and to get them to believe in you. One executive that has this attribute down is also one of my favorite clients. I have had the honor and privilege to work with, and witness, Chris Shockley as he moved up to the CEO position at his company. For this reason, I believe that Mr. Shockley can provide excellent insight into the benefit of showing competence as a leader.

Chris Shockley, President and CEO of the Virginia Credit Union, shared his perspective on **showing competence'** *as a rule when building employee trust.*

Being in the CEO role, I have a lot of diverse roles that report to me with a lot of expertise. For example, there is the role of CPA's. But within the CPA role they have different functions as well, such as a controller, CFO and internal auditors. All of these roles have different expectations. Another example is within our IT world. We have technologists. Some of our technologists focus on our mainframe, some are about our core system, while others are developers. It's just what I have faced working in the world of a smaller company.

In a bigger company I believe that you don't have to be as competent across a wide spectrum, you can be competent vertically. However, working in a company with 800 employees and associates, it's imperative to be more competent horizontally. For me, the lessons learned is knowing that employees have watched me learn from them to better understand their roles. I accomplished this by simply asking them to teach me.

In this leadership role, it is expected that you possess competence and know what is going on horizontally within the organization because as CEO you are attending one meeting after another. The management team participating in the meeting expects to have some confidence in you, as their leader, that there is some level of understanding of what they do on a daily basis.

Also, everyone on your team wants to be respected for the work they do. When you can harness that as a leader or manager, it will pay huge dividends. It's easy to be a leader when things go great but when things are tough, that's when competency of the job and business are truly needed.

Chris believes that you can begin to 'show your competence' as a leader by changing the perception of leading.

First, having the executive team understand that a vertical approach to leadership is not the ONLY way to lead. The vertical approach occurs when an executive is focusing solely on running their department such as lending, finance, contact center, marketing and products. In comparison, the horizontal approach is when the executive is thinking the impact of decisions across the different departments.

As an executive within an organization, it imperative that you have knowledge not just in your area of responsibility but also across the company. This is important because the decisions that you make are also perceived to be part of the 'executive team.' In reality 'competency' gets you to the executive table. For us as leaders, it's a new awareness of leading through a horizontal team approach which includes leaning on our colleagues.

Understanding that in order to grow, leaders have to think differently than where the company is currently. There is a need to think more strategically and critically. So, for us, the agenda is driven around how we're thinking about the future from an organizational view.

Here are some strategies that Chris uses at the Virginia Credit Union to **show competency** when building trust:

- Focus on inquiry, curiosity and questioning one another in meetings for professional and personal growth. Role model strategic thinking and competence for them by asking, "Do we have the right strategy and if not, what should it be?" "What should the new strategy evolve to?" and tying the discussion to the areas of leadership and accountability.

- Move beyond the 'data dump' approach to executive staff meetings that are tactile and operational. Spend time reading, researching and asking rich questions, not surface questions in meetings to build both your competence and team's competence. This can be accomplished by sharing a business article- read through it, and share the questions it inspired.

- Carve out time during the month for leadership development, such as trainings, webinars, or coaching.

- Focus on the 'Final 10.' As a leader, most are really good at giving constructive feedback. What's missing is the final 10%, which is the part that really helps everyone to become better as a group in order to move forward. The final 10% is the honesty needed to REALLY improve.

- Schedule monthly face-time with direct reports. Incorporate one-on-one discussions about performance and connect the dots to the strategic plan. Are we living out what we say we're committed to when it comes to helping our members live more confidently? It's important to tie our meetings back to the strategic plan so the team sees our purpose and that they 'get it.'

- Share news with leaders first so employees and managers aren't receiving company information at the same time. Let leaders be leaders. When sharing news with managers provide talking points or a guide so that there is a consistent message throughout the organization and prepared to answer.

- Visit every team and share with them how we run this company financially by sharing 'Get To Know The Business' videos.

- Deliver on what you've said you're going to do at breakfast/ communication meetings. I'm present for the team for any questions and show that accountability is important.

- Be honest. "When I don't know something, I admit I don't know it. I'm not worried about looking stupid. I am more concerned about understanding the person or situation. This encourages others to be more confident to ask questions and not fear looking stupid. Understand they as leaders can't know everything. In the end, asking questions improves job competency. I prefer to think that, "there are no stupid questions."

Chris believes that the #1 thing a leader should know about 'showing competence' to others is that *nobody cares how much you know unless you show how much you care. It's important to be humble enough to share that you care about them as a person and NOT just an employee. In the end, it's not about you as the leader, it's more about sharing what you know that will help them perform better at their job. It's also about learning together and really becoming a constant learner.*

Bottom-line.

It's my belief that employees really want to

- *find nobility in the work that they do*
- *feel valued for their contributions*
- *do a good job*
- *continue to learn and do well*
- *get opportunities to grow in their careers*

So, don't be selfish with your knowledge, it's no good if it's locked in your head.

When you stop thinking that you can be replaced and share your business knowledge, the employees will be more willing to do other things such as "other duties as assigned." Your employees' curiosity will come out as well when they start thinking about how they can improve upon their job role.

Provide opportunities for training and learning for others, but also remember to take advantage of training and learning yourself.

The final piece of advice that Chris would like to share is recognize that you never truly achieve full competence. There is always a nugget of information, that you didn't know before, that will help you improve what you're are doing today. As a leader, when you start giving yourself an excuse to not 'learn' by starting a sentence with "WELL" than you will never personally grow.

So, don't get stuck in the mindset that you no longer need to learn from colleagues, attend conferences, trainings or even some meetings. Know that you'd be missing out on the opportunity to learn.

Finally, don't forget to enjoy yourself along the way. You have to find joy in the work you do as a leader. If you are no longer getting fulfillment and joy in it, then stop doing it. In the end, you're killing others and you're killing yourself.

Magnetic Trust Rule #8: Don't Play Favorites

Looking back on all of the jobs that I have held, (it's only been 5,) I have to say there has only been ONE boss that played favorites. Thank goodness!

As a boss, you will see certain employees shine. A shining employee will be the one that shows up to work on time, (or early,) helps out other team members without being asked, always has a smile on his/her face, gives 110% effort on tasks, doesn't walk out the door before 5 p.m, etc.

Are you getting the picture?

Are you thinking of a specific employee right now who exhibits the characteristics of a 'perfect employee'?

You just love him or her don't you?

In comparison, you have an employee that may or may not shine as bright as that 'special' employee. Their personality may not mesh with yours, or they may consistently require more attention and direction than you feel is necessary, or you feel professionally threatened by their ability, or they find every excuse to NOT do their job. Whatever the case may be, you've decided this particular employee just doesn't meet the 'favorite' status like the first.

However, it's so important not to show a 'favorite' difference in how you delegate tasks, approve leave, award bonus, or pay increases.

In the end, playing the 'favorite' game hurts the rest of your team. When your employees watch you delegate projects, or award promotions to an underperforming employee, it negatively impacts morale, motivation and ultimately, TRUST.

Nancy DeLisi, Former Vice-President, Finance & Treasurer with Altria Group, Inc., shared her perspective on the importance of *not playing favorites with employees* and the impact it has when building Magnetic Trust.

Not 'playing favorites' with your employees is important for a lot of reasons that are similar to why you shouldn't play favorites as a parent. It's all about the relationship, and that you're supposed to be setting an example.

Nancy shares from her perspective that 'playing favorites doesn't work, just like making decisions based on being paternalistic. Just because an employee has a wife and three children, it doesn't mean they get rewarded with a promotion or bonus because of family obligations, versus rewarding based upon the merit system.

The merit-based leadership approach works very well as employees then begin to track their own performance. This is especially true in a 'paternalistic style' company where the younger manager may have less incentive to go over and above their job requirements.

The merit-based approach of leadership sends two messages:

1) *When employees have been in a company for many years, and they start to take advantage, and they think they have nothing to worry*

about, it sends a message across the bow that if you're going to come in late and leave early, you're not going to be rewarded.

2) *The younger employees now clearly understand that if they put in the hours needed to do the job, they get rewarded sooner rather than later. Their effort isn't wasted.*

It's at this point, Trust is developed, because they trust if they work hard, do what they are supposed to do, that there is a reward, and they trust that you are going to be fair.

Ultimately, this is what we are trying to do, and that is build trust and fairness within an organization.

So, how do you do it?

It's very simple, you reward and encourage on the merit-based system.

When you see an employee going the extra mile, you spend more time to help him to achieve his goals and objectives because you are the leader. It's not playing favorites, but rather, helping to optimize their potential.

I see that as very different than saying, "here is my buddy so he gets more opportunities." Instead, it's someone trying to achieve a certain goal and objective but needs a little more handholding because they are younger, with less experience.

Nancy believes that showing that you don't play favorites' as a leader with your employees is simple if you follow these strategies:

- Get the manager or supervisor to mentor the young employee that needs more 'handholding'. This creates trust with the supervisor or manager and allows the manager to be rewarded for doing their job. You are training him to be more of a leader.

- Treat everyone fairly based on criteria of goals and objectives. Those employees that achieve get rewarded, and the employees that don't, don't get rewarded.

- Communicate to managers what the expectations are, and make sure that gets translated down the ranks. This ensures all team members have NO DOUBT what the expectation level is.

- Meet with teams separately so they know what is happening, AND you can see what is happening. This allows opportunities for comments if they are getting derailed and provides positive feed-back when doing an incredibly good job.

- Encourage engagement so your team knows who YOU are, and knows how YOU think, so no one is blindsided at the end of the day. This is especially important in large organizations when you may have five or six different departments reporting to you.

- Delegate projects based upon merit and initiative to the person that has the skill set to get the job done, even though the level of experience might be lacking, but they possess the fire in the belly to get the job done. This provides a great learning experience for him or her if it is a low-risk project. It's not about who you like or don't like.

- Ask yourself if you are grooming and mentoring people (high potential person) by giving them low risk but important projects.

- Ask employees what their objectives are and during succession planning assess their strengths and level of readiness.

- Don't reward bad behavior for an employee that doesn't perform to the level of expectation. For instance, just because you go to lunch with an employee or play golf with them or they leave work early doesn't mean they get the merit raise, since they aren't working to their potential.

- Discourage your direct reports from rewarding incentives based upon perceived favorites.

Nancy believes the #1 thing a leader should know about 'not playing favorites' when building employee trust is: "Playing favorites in the long run doesn't work!

People do resent favoritism.

You aren't going to reach the objectives, and the 'favorites' aren't 'capable of carrying' out the task.

It creates a work environment that is unhealthy because they think, "I'll never get anywhere because I'm not the teacher's pet or the favorite." As a result, you may lose some very good people.

Under the merit-based system, employees who may otherwise be 'slacking off,' would just rise to the top, achieve objectives and make you as the leader look good.

In the end, having 'favorites' is detrimental to the person, to the leader, and to the company because you're not getting the best out of the group.

As a woman leader, the merit-based approached worked because the employees felt they were treated fairly.

Trust is built over time and based upon communication, engagement, and fair treatment.

Nancy's final piece of advice is that playing favorites doesn't help anyone.

In the end, friendships that drive 'showing favoritism' come to a very unhappy ending, and it creates an unhealthy environment because somewhere down the line, someone is going to notice it, and attempt to cover it up.

What Does All Of This Magnetic Trust Mean?

Congratulations.

As a busy business owner myself, I know how tough it is to carve out time to read any kind of book, much less a business book.

Well done.

My hope is that you take the Magnetic Trust building strategies that have been shared by some pretty smart business people and implement them within your company and team.

I personally want you to achieve the same company results that Gallup reported, of holding employee turnover to 10% or less annually, having 147% higher earnings and an 18% higher customer retention rate.

In closing - I encourage you to drop me a message at drheather@transformationgroupllc.com, visit my website at www.transformationgroupllc.com and attend one of my training webinars on Eventbrite in a city near you, to help you develop into the awesome leader I know you are inside.

Get out there and implement the Magnetic Trust strategies and keep me posted on your progress!

Much Success!

Dr. Heather

P.S. - If you enjoy this book or found it useful, I'll be very grateful if you post a short review on Amazon. Your support makes a difference and I read all the reviews personally so I can make this book even better.

About Dr. Heather Williamson

Originally from Clearwater, Florida, Dr. Heather found her leadership calling as an adult. While working in sales for Philip Morris USA, she had the opportunity to participate in two outward bound programs. It was through this experience, that she found her passion for leadership.

For Dr. Heather, it is about sharing her experience and expertise to help develop leaders to their full potential, so no employee has to experience an inadequate or mediocre manager.

She's a #1 Bestselling Author, Published Academic Author, Entrepreneur, Professor and says that her most important role is that of "mother."

She lives on her own little farm in Powhatan, Virginia with her husband and son, Temple.

Book Dr. Heather
To Speak

Hey there! It's Dr. Heather again. If you host events, (or know someone who does,) let's talk.

I absolutely love sharing my leadership message so that I can inspire and motivate others. So, if your corporation, association group, or non-profit is wanting to achieve change, then let's schedule a time to talk.

Full disclosure… I do this as a business. If you have a real budget and you want to hire a real speaker, let's talk.

For more information, and to book Dr. Heather for your next event, visit **drheather@tranformationgrou-pllc.com OR**, call +1 (804) 598-9175.

I can't wait to hear what you have going on, so don't forget to share the details.

Hiring Dr. Heather
For Coaching

One of the best ways to get the most out of your employees is by getting advice from someone who has been there, and done that.

My personal strength is coaching managers and leaders on how to get their employees to do the job they pay them to do.

I have also found in my years of experience, that your leadership staff does NOT want to talk to someone within your organization about management challenges for fear of retribution, or not being up to par, or oh yeah, trust that what is shared will remain confidential. That is why looking outside your organization is a much more effective strategy.

Some of the things we could work on together include...

- Executive Coaching
- Team Leadership
- Time Management
- Holding Employees Accountable
- Improving processes
- Strategic Thinking
- Succession Planning
- Team Building
- Management Training
- Customer Loyalty

So, if you are interested in coaching with me or putting me on retainer in your organization, shoot me an email at drheather@transformationgroupllc.com.

Social Media

If you want to follow me and get the BEST leadership tips and strategies then follow me on social media.

Check me out at….

Facebook:

https://www.facebook.com/drheatherwilliamson/
(Business Page)

Facebook:

https://www.facebook.com/groups/transformation-albusinessleaders (Private Group)

LinkedIn:

https://www.linkedin.com/in/drheatherwilliamson/

Appendix A

8 MAGNETIC TRUST RULES TO IMPLEMENT WITHIN YOUR COMPANY

Here is a check list of the Magnetic Trust Rules shared within this book. I purposely wanted to make sure you had a check list with action steps that you can take back to your office to make your life a little easier.

MAGNETIC TRUST RULE #1:
BE AUTHENTIC

- Make yourself vulnerable. (easier said than done I know) If you don't know the answer, say you don't know.

- Own your mistakes when made and apologize, (this isn't the norm,) but it allows people to see that you are human.

- Allow people not to be perfect by providing a safe environment to learn from their mistakes.

- Let people know it's OK not to play it SAFE.

- Allow the team to share opinions, don't just say it because you are their administrator or boss.

- Give credit for contributions and opinions when suggestions are implemented.

- Emphasize when you don't have all of the answers, so, be open to welcoming feedback.

MAGNETIC TRUST RULE #2: BE PREDICTABLE

- Set clear expectations, so that your employees clearly understand what you want from them.

- Be available at the same time, not necessarily all the time but at consistent times.

- Treat each person and situation consistently.

- Follow-up with a handwritten note afterwards whenever you meet or call a staff member.

- Be available. Be clear when you're not available and what to do if you are not there in those instances. Also, when you are out of the office or in meetings, let your people know who to contact for solutions.

- Hold regularly scheduled meetings and make sure you share the agenda ahead of time in both team and individual meetings. Be sure to share input of what is happening in the company and not have surprises.

- Keep the same demeanor when someone comes with a situation by turning off what is in your head, and focus on them exclusively. Make them feel like they are the only one in the room. This can be accomplished by turning away from computer and putting away the cell phone when you meet.

MAGNETIC TRUST RULE #3:
BE TRANSPARENT

- Be transparent and clear in terms of all goals (i.e., revenue, market share, sales, product).

- Be transparent on company challenges such as being #2 in the market.

- Be transparent on performance and how you are being measured. (It involves trust and partnership).

- Have the mindset and internal strength to exhibit a 'What you see is what you get' transparency.

MAGNETIC TRUST RULE #4: EXHIBIT ETHICS

- Hold management meetings every two months and talking about the good, bad and ugly. These discussions should include what you are doing really well, where you are falling short and need to incorporate corrective action plans and finally identify specific areas that are not meeting standards.

- Take the opportunity to explain why certain decisions are being made and listening to the perspectives of employees and answering their questions, being available for, and taking the jabs when needed.

- Exhibit ethical behavior. Remember there are thousands of eyeballs watching what you do and listening to what you say. As a leader, you're a teacher no matter what, and always "ON." Your staff watches what you say, and watches what you do, and then decides on that basis how to act.

- Talk with leadership and employees consistently.

- Recognize the importance that everyone brings to the job, no matter what level. Stop and shake hands and thank everyone for their contributions.

- Be a cheerleader for the team. Communicate constant positive reinforcement, walk around the office, plant yourself in one spot, then change walking patterns, and bring others to share in the 'walk' and share their observations.

- Teach people the right way to go so they are successful. Incorporate continuous learning as part of your principles. Even make discipline productive by turning it into a teaching opportunity by making the behavior change clear.

- Be enthusiastic by doing cheers, reminding people that enthusiasm is contagious. As a method to achieve enthusiasm, we incorporate jumping jacks, pushups, and other shared team experiences as activities to build our team.

MAGNETIC TRUST RULE #5: COMMUNICATE, COMMUNICATE, COMMUNICATE

- When a question arises, get out of your chair, and going to the employee for clarification, allowing a face-to-face conversation, rather than sending emails, which can cause more confusion.

- When holding weekly staff meetings, make it a point NEVER to do all of the talking. The focus is on the staff and they would share what they are working on, feelings of success, current challenges, and finally what they are feeling overwhelmed about.

- Provide team building exercises yearly so the team learns one another's strengths and weaknesses.

- Schedule time out of the office for lunch to celebrate birthdays and project successes so that we could bond and better understand each other outside the office.

- Encourage staff to know it's OK to have conversations when experiencing challenges.

- Include entire non-profit staff to attend board meetings when possible as it's beneficial that everyone hears the same message.

- Communicate board goals so everyone is on board to be a cohesive team.
- Customer service- put your best hat on to be attentive to the ask or concern for anyone that called or walked through the door.

MAGNETIC TRUST RULE #6: OWN IT, DON'T BLAME IT

- Be very 'hands on' and present with your team. Show empathy in what is needed to get the job done but don't do their job.

- Walk around the 1st hour of the morning, and talking to your team, and help out when you see an employee struggling.

- Lead by example. When they see me helping the team, I hope that next time an employee may exhibit the same behaviors, by helping others when needed.

- Encourage the team to be brave and think outside the box to make their job easier while supporting their ideas when finding better ways to do things. If the ideas are good ones, then support them by allocating resources.

MAGNETIC TRUST RULE #7: SHOW COMPETENCE

- Focus on inquiry, curiosity and questioning one another in meetings for professional and personal growth. Role model strategic thinking and competence for them by asking, "Do we have the right strategy and if not, what should it be?" "What should the new strategy evolve to?" and tying the discussion to the areas of leadership and accountability.

- Move beyond the 'data dump' approach to executive staff meetings that are tactile and operational. Spend time reading, researching and asking rich questions, not surface questions in meetings to build both your competence and team's competence.

- Carve out time during the month for leadership development, such as trainings, webinars, or coaching.

- Focus on the 'Final 10.' As a leader, most are really good at giving constructive feedback. What's missing is the final 10%, which is the part that really helps everyone to become better as a group in order to move forward.

- Schedule monthly face-time with direct reports. Incorporate one-on-one discussions about performance and connect the dots to the strategic plan.

- Share news with leaders first so employees and managers aren't receiving company information at the same time. Let leaders be leaders. When sharing news with managers provide talking points or a guide so that there is a consistent message throughout the organization and prepared to answer.

- Visit every team and share with them how we run this company financially by sharing 'Get To Know The Business' videos.

- Deliver on what you've said you're going to do at breakfast/ communication meetings.

- Be honest. "When I don't know something, I admit I don't know it. I'm not worried about looking stupid. I am more concerned about understanding the person or situation.

MAGNETIC TRUST RULE #8: DON'T PLAY FAVORITES

- Get the manager or supervisor to mentor the young employee that needs more 'handholding'.

- Treat everyone fairly based on criteria of goals and objectives. Those employees that achieve get rewarded, and the employees that don't, don't get rewarded.

- Communicate to managers what the expectations are, and make sure that gets translated down the ranks.

- Meet with teams separately so they know what is happening, AND you can see what is happening.

- Encourage engagement so your team knows who YOU are, and knows how YOU think, so no one is blindsided at the end of the day.

- Delegate projects based upon merit and initiative to the person that has the skill set to get the job done, even though the level of experience might be lacking, but they possess the fire in the belly to get the job done.

- Ask yourself if you are grooming and mentoring people (high potential person) by giving them low risk but important projects.

- Ask employees what their objectives are and during succession planning assess their strengths and level of readiness.

- Don't reward bad behavior for an employee that doesn't perform to the level of expectation.

- Discourage your direct reports from rewarding incentives based upon perceived favorites.

39585988R00060

Made in the USA
Middletown, DE
22 March 2019